Welcome To

ADVENTURES IN ANGEL FIRE, NM

Adult Coloring Book

I Hope You Enjoy This Book
As It Will Bring You Many
Hours Of Stress-free Time!

Enjoy Wonderful And Relaxing
Illustration, All Related To The Area.

Illustrations by: Shahin Mahmud

SPARKY THE WONDER DOG

THANK YOU FOR PURCHASING

PLEASE HURRY BACK FOR MORE FUN!

Remember

The Best Yet To Come!
"GOD BLESS YOU"